This copy of

O Lord, Hear My Prayer

comes to

....

with love from

....

Copyright © 1998, Eagle
British Library Cataloguing-in-Publication Data. A catalogue record for
this book is available from the British Library.
Published by Eagle, an imprint of Inter Publishing Service (IPS) Ltd, St
Nicholas House, 14 The Mount, Guildford, Surrey GU2 5HN.
Scripture quotations are taken from the following versions: NIV, *New
International Version*; JER, *Jerusalem Bible*; RSV, *Revised Standard Version*;
GNB, *Good News Bible*.

Typeset by Eagle
Printed in Singapore
ISBN: 0 86347 261 3

O LORD,
HEAR MY PRAYER

PRAYERS FOR EVERY DAY

eagle

Guildford, Surrey

My soul yearns for you

You will keep in perfect peace
    him whose mind is steadfast,
    because he trusts in you . . .
O upright One, you make the way of the
    righteous smooth.
Yes, LORD, walking in the way of your laws,
    we wait for you;
your name and renown
    are the desire of our hearts.
My soul yearns for you in the night;
    in the morning my spirit longs for you.

                           Isaiah 26:3,7–9, NIV

Fishing by the Bridge, Henry John Yeend King

I remember you in my prayers

I remember you in my prayers and ask the God of our LORD Jesus Christ, the glorious Father, to give you the Spirit, who will make you wise and reveal God to you, so that you will know him. I ask that your minds may be opened to see his light, so that you will know what is the hope to which he has called you, how rich are the wonderful blessings he promises his people, and how very great is his power at work in us who believe.

Ephesians 1:16–19, GNB

Picking Buttercups, Helen Allingham

You are my God

O God, you are my God,
    earnestly I seek you;
my soul thirsts for you,
my body longs for you,
in a dry and weary land
    where there is no water.
I have seen you in the sanctuary
    and beheld your power and your glory.
Because your love is better than life,
    my lips will glorify you.
I will praise you as long as I live,
    and in your name I will lift up my hands.
My soul will be satisfied as with the richest of
      foods;
    with singing lips my mouth will praise you.
On my bed I remember you;
    I think of you through the watches of the
      night.
Because you are my help,
    I sing in the shadow of your wings.
My soul clings to you;
    your right hand upholds me.

Psalm 63:1–8, NIV

Poppies on the Riverbank, Ernest Walbourne

Your right hand will hold me fast

LORD, you have examined me and you know me.
You know everything I do;
    from far away you understand all my
      thoughts.
You see me, whether I am working or resting;
    you know all my actions.
Even before I speak,
    you already know what I will say.
You are all round me on every side;
    you protect me with your power.
Your knowledge of me is too deep;
    it is beyond my understanding.
Where could I go to escape from you?
    Where could I get away from your presence? . . .

If I flew away beyond the east,
    or lived in the furthest place in the west,
You would be there to lead me,
    you would be there to help me.

Psalm 139:1–7,9,10, GNB

Gleaning, Arthur Foord Hughes

I call to you, Lord

I call to you, Lord; help me now!
  Listen to me when I call to you.
Receive my prayer as incense,
  my uplifted hands as an evening sacrifice.
Lord, place a guard at my mouth,
  a sentry at the door of my lips.
Keep me from wanting to do wrong
  and from joining evil men in their wickedness.
May I never take part in their feasts.

Psalm 141:1–4, GNB

'As the Twig is bent, so the Tree is inclined',
James Hayllar

My heart is quiet within me

LORD, I have given up my pride
  and turned away from my arrogance.
I am not concerned with great matters
  or with subjects too difficult for me.
As a child lies quietly in its mother's arms,
  so my heart is quiet within me.
Israel, trust in the LORD
  now and forever!

Psalm 131:1–3, GNB

Mother's Lesson, George Washington Brownlow

The LORD is king

The LORD is king.
>   He is clothed with majesty and strength.
The earth is set firmly in place
>   and cannot be moved.
Your throne, O LORD, has been firm from the
>   beginning,
>   and you existed before time began.

The oceans raise their voice, O LORD;
>   they raise their voice and roar.
The LORD rules supreme in heaven,
>   greater than the roar of the ocean,
>   more powerful than the waves of the sea.

Your laws are eternal, LORD,
>   and your Temple is holy indeed,
>   for ever and ever.

Psalm 93:1–5, GNB

Cullercoats Cliffs, Myles Birket Foster

Teach me your ways

LORD, you have given us your laws
    and told us to obey them faithfully.
How I hope that I shall be faithful
    in keeping your instructions!
If I pay attention to all your commands,
    then I will not be put to shame.
As I learn your righteous judgments,
    I will praise you with a pure heart.
I will obey your laws;
    never abandon me! . . .
With all my heart I try to serve you;
    keep me from disobeying your commandments.
I keep your law in my heart,
    so that I will not sin against you.
I praise you, O LORD;
    teach me your ways.

Psalm 119:4–8,10–12, GNB

A Helpful Sister, Edith Hume

O LORD, let your ear be attentive

O LORD, God of heaven, the great and awesome
God, who keeps his covenant of love with those
who love him and obey his commands, let your
ear be attentive and your eyes open to hear the
prayer your servant is praying before you day
and night for your servants . . .
Remember the instruction you gave your servant
Moses, saying, 'If you are unfaithful, I will scatter
you among the nations, but if you return to me
and obey my commands, then even if your exiled
people are at the farthest horizon, I will gather
them from there and bring them to the place I
have chosen as a dwelling for My name.' . . .

O LORD, let your ear be attentive . . .
Nehemiah 1:5,6,8–9,11, NIV

Daydreams, Marcus Stone

I will call on him

I love the LORD, for he heard my voice;
    he heard my cry for mercy.
Because he turned his ear to me,
    I will call on him as long as I live . . .

For you, O LORD, have delivered my soul from
      death,
    my eyes from tears,
    my feet from stumbling,
that I may walk before the LORD
    in the land of the living.
I believed; therefore I said,
    'I am greatly afflicted.' . . .

Praise the LORD.

                Psalm 116:1,2,8–10,17–19, NIV

At a Cottage Door, Helen Allingham

Save me, O God

Save me, God! The water
    is already up to my neck!

I am sinking in the deepest swamp,
    there is no foothold;
I have stepped into deep water
    and the waves are washing over me.

Worn out with calling, my throat is hoarse,
my eyes are strained, looking for my God . . .

God, you know how foolish I have been,
my offences are not hidden from you . . .

For my part, I pray to you, Yahweh,
    at the time you wish;
in your great love, answer me, God,
    faithful in saving power.
Rescue me from the mire,
    do not let me sink; . . .

In your loving kindness, answer me, Yahweh,
    in your great tenderness turn to me;
do not hide your face from your servant,
    quick, I am in trouble, answer me;
come to my side, redeem me . . .

Psalm 69:1–3, 5,6,13–14,16–18, JER

Willows on the Ouse, William Fraser Garden

In you, O LORD, I have taken refuge

In you, O LORD, I have taken refuge;
    let me never be put to shame.
Rescue me and deliver me in your righteousness;
    turn your ear to me and save me.
Be my rock of refuge,
    to which I can always go . . .

For you have been my hope, O Sovereign LORD,
    my confidence since my youth.
From my birth I have relied on you;
    you brought me forth from my mother's womb.
    I will ever praise you . . .

Do not cast me away when I am old;
    do not forsake me when my strength is gone . . .

But as for me, I shall always have hope;
    I will praise you more and more.
My mouth will tell of your righteousness,
    of your salvation all day long,
    though I know not its measure.
I will come and proclaim your mighty acts, O
       Sovereign LORD; . . .
Since my youth, O God, you have taught me,
    and to this day I declare your marvellous deeds.
                Psalm 71:1–3,5,6,9,14–17, NIV

Good News From Abroad, George Smith

I will meditate on all your works

I will remember the works of the LORD;
Surely I will remember Your wonders of old.
I will also meditate on all Your work,
And talk of Your deeds.

Your way, O God, is in the sanctuary;
Who is so great a God as our God?
You are the God who does wonders;
You have declared Your strength among the
    peoples.

                        Psalm 77:11–14, NKJV

Les Fleurs du Printemps, Arthur Hacker

Give me understanding

Teach me, O LORD, to follow your decrees;
    then I will keep them to the end.
Give me understanding, and I will keep your law
    and obey it with all my heart.
Direct me in the path of your commands,
    for there I find delight.
Turn my heart towards your statutes
    and not towards selfish gain.
Turn my eyes away from worthless things;
    preserve my life according to your word.
                      Psalm 119:33–37, NIV

Feeding the Calves, Ernest Walbourne

Picture Credits

Eagle Publishing is grateful to the The Fine Art Picture
Library who hold copyright for all the illustrations, unless
otherwise indicated, for their kind permission to reproduce
the paintings selected to complement the text.

cover *Les Fleurs du Printemps,* Arthur Hacker (1858-1919)
1 *Fishing by the Bridge,* Henry John Yeend King (1855-1924)
2 *Picking Buttercups,* Helen Allingham (1848-1926), courtesy
  Bourne Gallery
3 *Poppies on the Riverbank,* Ernest Walbourne (1897-1927?),
  courtesy Christopher Cole Paintings
4 *Gleaning,* Arthur Foord Hughes (1856-1927)
5 *'As the Twig is bent, so the Tree is inclined',* James Hayllar
  (1829-1920), courtesy Christopher Wood Gallery
6 *Mother's Lesson,* George Washington Brownlow (1858-
  1875), courtesy Bourne Gallery
7 *Cullercoats Cliffs,* Myles Birket Foster (1825-1899)
8 *A Helpful Sister,* Edith Hume (1862-1992), courtesy Polak
  Gallery
9 *Daydreams,* Marcus Stone (1840-1921)
10 *At a Cottage Door,* Helen Allingham (1848-1926),
   copyright Eagle
11 *Willows on the Ouse,* William Fraser Garden (1856-1921),
   courtesy Christopher Wood Gallery
12 *Good News From Abroad,* George Smith (1829-1901)
13 *Les Fleurs du Printemps,* Arthur Hacker (1858-1919)
14 *Feeding the Calves,* Ernest Walbourne (1897-1904)